BREAD MACHINE

Bread Machine Cookbook for Beginners

A Simple Recipe Book with Gluten-Free Recipes for Home DIY Baking Using Your Bread Maker

Sierra A. May

BREAD MACHINE COOKBOOK

Bluesource And Friends

This book is brought to you by Bluesource And Friends, a happy book publishing company.

Our motto is **"Happiness Within Pages"**

We promise to deliver amazing value to readers with our books.

We also appreciate honest book reviews from our readers.

Connect with us on our Facebook page www.facebook.com/bluesourceandfriends and stay tuned to our latest book promotions and free giveaways.

BREAD MACHINE COOKBOOK

© Copyright 2020 - All rights reserved.

The content contained within this book may not be reproduced, duplicated nor transmitted without direct written permission from the author or the publisher.

Under no circumstances will any blame or legal responsibility be held against the publisher, or author, for any damages, reparation, or monetary loss due to the information contained within this book, either directly or indirectly.

Legal Notice:

This book is copyright-protected. It is only for personal use. You cannot amend, distribute, sell, use, quote or paraphrase any part, or the content within this book, without the consent of the author or publisher.

Disclaimer Notice:

Please note that the information contained within this document is for educational and entertainment purposes only. All effort has been executed to present accurate, up to date, reliable, complete information. No warranties of any kind are declared or implied. Readers acknowledge that the author is not engaged in the rendering of legal, financial, medical or professional advice. The content within this book has been derived from various sources. Please consult a licensed professional before attempting any techniques outlined in this book.

BREAD MACHINE COOKBOOK

By reading this document, the reader agrees that under no circumstances is the author responsible for any losses, direct or indirect, that are incurred as a result of the use of the information contained within this document, including, but not limited to, errors, omissions, or inaccuracies.

BREAD MACHINE COOKBOOK

Table of Contents

Introduction: Cooking with Your Bread Maker........8

Chapter 1: Why Use a Bread Maker?......................11

    The Benefits of Using a Bread Maker 13

    Tips on How to Use and Maintain Your Bread Maker................15

Chapter 2: Making Different Types of Gluten-Free Bread 19

    Why Gluten-Free? 19

    Deli-Style Bread 24

    White Bread................27

    Buckwheat Bread 29

    Garlic Bread................31

    Multigrain Bread 34

    Ciabatta Bread 38

    Sourdough Bread................41

    Olive and Onion Bread................44

Chapter 3: Making Sweet Bread Loaves................46

    Pumpernickel Loaf................46

    Banana Pumpkin Loaf................50

    Honey Oat Loaf................52

BREAD MACHINE COOKBOOK

    Cinnamon Loaf with Raisins 54

    Pull-Apart Lemony Bread...............57

    Making Recipes Gluten-Free 60

Chapter 4: Getting Creative with Pastries 64

    Bagels 64

    Chocolate Chip Brioche...............68

    Soft Pretzels 71

    Challah............74

    Donuts 77

Chapter 5: Surprising Things You Can Cook in Your Bread Maker 80

    Meatloaf 80

    Fresh Fruit Jams 83

    Butternut Squash Soup 87

    Mushroom and Cranberry Risotto 89

    Peach Cobbler............91

Conclusion: Let's Get Cooking!............94

Bluesource And Friends 95

BREAD MACHINE COOKBOOK

Introduction: Cooking with Your Bread Maker

As a mom (or dad), have you ever wondered how you can make your time in the kitchen more interesting? If you're tired of the old pots and pans, then you might want to consider purchasing a bread maker. There is nothing like starting your day with freshly-baked bread that you have made with your own two hands and the help of a convenient, versatile kitchen appliance.

Most people choose to buy their bread from stores because baking bread from scratch takes a lot of time, effort, and practice. In fact, most people won't even try to make their own bread because they feel like it's too difficult. But thanks to the bread maker or bread machine, you can make simple, gluten-free bread loaves and so much more. The great thing about baking your bread from home is that you can choose all of the ingredients that go into your culinary masterpiece. This means that if you are on a strict diet—like if you have chosen to go gluten-free—you

BREAD MACHINE COOKBOOK

won't have to worry about what you are putting on the table.

In this eBook, you will learn several gluten-free bread recipes along with a couple of unique recipes that will make you feel pleasantly surprised. If you have a bread maker in your kitchen and you have no idea how to use it, you will learn how to use it here. If you don't own a bread maker yet but you're thinking of buying one, this eBook will help you make a wise choice. You will also learn more about this unique kitchen appliance and how you can make virtually any recipe gluten-free.

By the end of this eBook, you will be able to impress your friends and family with all of the new dishes you serve them, all of which are made in your bread maker. But before we begin, you should know that different bread makers come with different features and functions. The best way for you to create amazing bread in your appliance (along with other clever dishes) is by learning about the bread maker you have sitting on your countertop.

If you haven't purchased a bread maker yet, this eBook will help you make the best choice as you would know what to look for in terms of options and features. If you're on a gluten-free diet, then you may

BREAD MACHINE COOKBOOK

want to opt for a bread maker that is specifically designed for gluten-free bread. Also, if you would like to cook more than just bread (yes, it's possible!) in your bread maker, then look for one which offers different functions.

At the end of the day, we all want to serve the healthiest and tastiest dishes to our families. Although a bread maker might seem like a one-dimensional, simple appliance, you are about to find out that this isn't the case. If you're ready to learn everything you can about your bread maker—plus some healthy, gluten-free recipes—then let's get cooking!

Chapter 1: Why Use a Bread Maker?

A bread maker or bread machine is a type of kitchen appliance that is primarily used to bake different types of bread. This appliance includes a bread pan, detachable paddles, and a special oven that does the baking and cooking. Essentially, a bread maker is a small electric oven. But even if this appliance is called a bread maker and most people use it to bake bread, the cooking possibilities don't stop there.

Apart from bread and bread loaves, you can make many other dishes in your bread maker. While bread makers are versatile appliances, your ability to cook a wide range of dishes will depend on the type of bread maker you have. All bread makers share the same functions, but there are some models that have special features that allow you to create more complex recipes. Some of the most common types of bread makers are:

- **Large**—which is the most practical option if you have a family and you all enjoy eating bread. This type of bread maker can produce

BREAD MACHINE COOKBOOK

loaves of up to three pounds, which makes them perfect for big families.
- **Small**—the most practical option if you seldom eat bread or if you have limited space in your kitchen. Usually, the bread it makes would be enough for just one or two people.
- **Horizontal**—where the bread pan is positioned horizontally. This type creates horizontal bread loaves and typically comes with two paddles for kneading.
- **Vertical**—where the bread pan is positioned vertically. This type creates vertical bread loaves and typically comes with a single paddle for kneading.
- **Gluten-Free**—which are specifically meant for those following a gluten-free diet. If you are on this type of diet and you haven't bought a bread maker yet, you might want to choose a gluten-free bread maker so that you can create gluten-free bread and other recipes with ease.

No matter what type of bread maker you have, the one thing these appliances have in common is that you can use them for different purposes—not just for baking.

BREAD MACHINE COOKBOOK

The Benefits of Using a Bread Maker

Most people have forgotten how to make bread the "traditional way," especially now when it's much easier and more convenient to buy your bread loaves from the supermarket. But if you have a bread maker at home, you can easily bake your own bread since there is nothing like freshly-baked bread for you and your kids to enjoy. If you still aren't convinced, here are some benefits of using a bread maker:

- **It's Very Simple to Use**

  As you will come to discover, cooking or baking with a bread maker typically involves adding all of the ingredients at one go. Then you just close the lid and choose the right setting. Simplicity is one of the most important benefits of using a bread maker that all users appreciate.

- **You Can Make High-Quality Bread at Home**

BREAD MACHINE COOKBOOK

No matter what diet you're on, you can choose all of the ingredients that go into the bread you bake. By baking your own bread, you can opt for the best ingredients so that you can be sure that everything you serve to your kids is healthy, tasty, and of the highest quality.

- **It's More Economical**

    While it might seem cheaper to buy bread from the supermarket, purchasing ingredients for different types of bread is more economical in the long run.

- **Other Benefits**

    Apart from their simplicity, the ability to make healthier bread, and its money saving potential, using a bread maker to make fresh bread (and other dishes) comes with other advantages including:

    - It allows you to avoid preservatives, additives, and other chemicals that are usually found in processed-bread products.
    - It allows you to stick with your family's special diet. For instance, you

BREAD MACHINE COOKBOOK

> can use your bread maker to create gluten-free bread, pastries, and other dishes.
> - You can use a bread maker even if you don't have plenty of culinary skills or experience.
> - You can bake fresh bread whenever you want, which, in turn, helps you avoid food waste.
> - You can make different types of bread—even types that you haven't tried in the past!

As you can see, it's truly beneficial to own a bread maker. Now that you know why you should start using this clever appliance, let's move on to how you can use it properly.

Tips on How to Use and Maintain Your Bread Maker

If you try to read the instruction manual of your bread maker, you will realize that using it is a breeze. Of course, there are certain things you can do to

BREAD MACHINE COOKBOOK

ensure that you're using this appliance correctly and possibly extend its lifespan. Here are some healthy pointers on how to get the most out of your bread maker:

- **Learn All About the Model You Own**

    Before you start using your bread maker, the most important thing you must do is learn all about it. You can go through the manual of your bread maker or you can go online and learn about it. Familiarizing yourself with the bread maker that you have in your kitchen will allow you to use it properly no matter what type of bread or dish you are planning to whip up.

- **Know Your Bread Maker's Capacity**

    Knowing the capacity of your bread maker allows you to make adjustments to recipes as needed. That way, you don't end up adding too many ingredients to the bread pan of your bread maker. Doing this might overwhelm your appliance. Knowing how much flour you should add is particularly important.

- **Familiarize Yourself With the Order of Ingredients Your Bread Maker Requires**

BREAD MACHINE COOKBOOK

As you will soon discover, the order by which you add the ingredients to your bread maker depends on the model that you own. This is one of the things to take note of when you are learning about your appliance.

- **Follow Recipes Exactly**

This is very important, especially since you will simply add all of the ingredients into your bread maker. If you see that the recipe will make a loaf of bread that your appliance cannot handle, make the adjustments as needed. This will ensure that the bread or pastries that you bake will come out as expected.

- **Be aware of the things that will ruin your bread maker**

There are a few mistakes a lot of people make that end up ruining their bread makers. To ensure that your bread maker lasts for years to come, avoid the following:

  - Overwhelming your bread maker by adding more ingredients than it can handle, especially in terms of flour.
  - Not using fresh yeast in your recipes.

BREAD MACHINE COOKBOOK

- Not reading and following the recipes exactly.

Now that you have a better idea of how to use your bread maker properly, it's time to start baking! The next chapters are all about gluten-free bread maker recipes along with a few tips for you to help you stick with your gluten-free diet.

Chapter 2: Making Different Types of Gluten-Free Bread

These days, one of the trendiest diets is the gluten-free diet. This diet is especially important for people who suffer from specific medical conditions or food sensitivities. If you and other members of your family must avoid gluten to stay healthy, then it's important for you to learn how to bake and cook different recipes that are free of this special type of protein. Now that you know more about your bread maker and how to use it, the next thing you must learn is how to make gluten-free bread in your bread maker. But before that, let's look at the reasons why you should opt for a gluten-free diet in the first place.

Why Gluten-Free?

Gluten is a type of protein that is found in rye, barley, and wheat. For most people, gluten doesn't pose a problem. However, certain health conditions might

BREAD MACHINE COOKBOOK

require you to avoid gluten. In fact, if you or any of your family members suffer from such health conditions, consuming gluten can have harmful effects. If you're interested in following a gluten-free diet or you're considering it, here are the most important reasons why you should go gluten-free:

- **You Suffer From Gluten Sensitivity**

    If you have gluten sensitivity, consumption of foods that contain this protein may cause damage to your body. Although the damage isn't significant, consuming gluten repeatedly can take a toll on your body. The effects of gluten on your body will depend on the level of sensitivity you have to this protein. If you are diagnosed with this condition, it's best to avoid gluten altogether.

- **Gluten Promotes Inflammation in the Body**

    Unfortunately, gluten also has inflammatory properties. If you already suffer from gluten sensitivity or other inflammatory conditions, consuming foods that contain gluten might exacerbate those conditions. Therefore, going gluten-free might improve your quality of life.

BREAD MACHINE COOKBOOK

- **You Suffer From Celiac Disease**

  This is a type of autoimmune disease wherein the consumption of gluten triggers your immune system to start attacking your small intestines. Sadly, if you suffer from celiac disease, consuming even minimal amounts of gluten can have significant negative effects. To prevent these effects, you would have to follow a strict gluten-free diet. Among all the reasons to go gluten-free, this one is the most important.

- **You Suffer From Irritable Bowel Syndrome (IBS)**

  According to some studies, people who suffer from IBS can find relief by going gluten-free. This is another condition that can improve by following a gluten-free diet, whether it is you who suffers from it or someone else in your family.

- **Foods That Contain Gluten Aren't Nutrient-dense**

  Even if you don't have to go gluten-free because you suffer from a medical condition, avoiding foods that contain this protein won't

BREAD MACHINE COOKBOOK

affect your health significantly. This is because food items that contain gluten aren't nutrient-dense anyway. It's better to opt for gluten-free options that offer more vitamins, minerals, and nutrients for yourself and the rest of your family.

- **Gluten Tends to Block the Body's Absorption of Nutrients**

  Finally, the consumption of gluten can also block your body's ability to absorb nutrients, especially if you suffer from the aforementioned conditions. In such a case, consumption of gluten might lead to another condition known as "leaky gut syndrome", which comes with its own host of adverse side effects.

As you can see, there are several important reasons why going gluten-free is an excellent step in the right direction in terms of your health. If you're ready to start making gluten-free bread for your family using your bread machine, here are some simple recipes to start with.

Please note that the cooking time and total times of these recipes are estimates based on average bread

BREAD MACHINE COOKBOOK

makers. You should check your bread maker's instructions to confirm the proper cooking times for your particular model.

BREAD MACHINE COOKBOOK

Deli-Style Bread

This homemade gluten-free bread recipe is also dairy-free and very simple to make. If you're planning to make sandwiches for lunch or dinner, this bread would be perfect for your family's meal. It has an amazing texture, tastes great, and you can pair it with different fillings based on what your family is craving for.

Nutritional Information: 162 calories per serving

Time: 1 hour and 20 minutes

Servings Made: 16

Prep Time: 15 minutes

Cook Time: 1 hour and 5 minutes

Ingredients:

- 1 tsp apple cider vinegar
- 1 tsp baking powder
- 1 tsp salt
- 2 ¼ tsp dry active yeast
- 2 ½ tsp xanthan gum

BREAD MACHINE COOKBOOK

- 2 tbsp sugar (you can also use honey)
- ¼ cup of avocado oil (you can also use an oil of your choice)
- ¼ cup of ground flaxseed
- ½ cup of millet flour (you can also use almond flour)
- ¾ cup of potato starch (you can also use arrowroot starch)
- ¾ cup of tapioca starch
- 1 cup of white rice flour
- 1 ¼ cup of water (the temperature must be between 95°F to 110°F)
- 3 eggs (whites only)

Directions:

- In the pan of your bread machine, add the oil, apple cider vinegar, egg whites, and water.
- In a bowl, combine the white rice flour, tapioca starch, potato starch, millet flour, flaxseed, xanthan gum, baking powder, salt, and sugar then whisk together well.
- Add the dry-ingredient mixture to the pan of your bread machine over the mixture of wet ingredients.
- Use your finger to make a well in the middle of the mound of dry ingredients.

BREAD MACHINE COOKBOOK

- Add the dry yeast inside the well, making sure that it doesn't touch the wet mixture.
- Cancel your bread machine's "rest" setting if it has one.
- Choose the "gluten-free" setting on your bread machine, close the lid, and then press the "start" button.
- Once baked, take the bread loaf out of your bread machine and allow it to cool down before slicing.

BREAD MACHINE COOKBOOK

White Bread

This basic recipe is made with gluten-free ingredients. This is the simplest type of bread that you can make at home. This recipe is made with easy-to-find ingredients that you can get at your local supermarket.

Nutritional Information: 242 calories per serving

Time: 1 hour and 40 minutes to 1 hour and 50 minutes

Servings Made: 12

Prep Time: 10 minutes

Cook Time: 1 hour and 30 minutes to 1 hour and 40 minutes (This is an estimate based on average bread makers. Check your bread maker's instructions to confirm the proper time.)

Ingredients:

- 1 tsp salt
- 1 tbsp active dry yeast
- 1 tbsp cider vinegar
- 1 tbsp xanthan gum

BREAD MACHINE COOKBOOK

- ¼ cup of honey
- ¼ cup of olive oil
- ⅓ cup of cornstarch
- ½ cup of potato starch
- ½ cup of soy flour
- 1 ½ cups of buttermilk (room temperature)
- 2 cups of white rice flour
- 3 eggs

Directions:

- Check the manufacturer's instructions of your bread machine and add the ingredients to the bread pan accordingly. Usually, you would have to add the wet ingredients first then the dry ones.
- Choose the sweet dough cycle on your bread machine.
- After 5 minutes, open your bread machine and check the dough's consistency. If needed, add more liquid or flour to get the right consistency.
- Once cooked, take the bread pan out of your bread machine and allow it to cool for about 15 minutes before you remove the bread loaf from the pan.

Buckwheat Bread

This unique type of bread takes some practice since gluten helps it rise. But if you're a fan of buckwheat bread, you'll be happy to know that this recipe has been tried and tested—and it works even without gluten. As long as you follow the directions of this recipe, you can get amazing results.

Nutritional Information: Approximately 660 calories per serving

Time: 2 hours and 30 minutes

Servings Made: 12

Prep Time: 10 minutes

Cook Time: 2 hours and 30 minutes to 2 hours and 40 minutes (This is an estimate based on average bread makers. Check your bread maker's instructions to confirm the proper time.)

Ingredients:

- 1 tsp sea salt
- 1 tsp soy lecithin

BREAD MACHINE COOKBOOK

- 1 tbsp active dry yeast
- 1 tbsp xanthan gum
- 3 tbsp butter (softened)
- ½ cup of buckwheat flour
- ½ cup of potato starch
- ½ cup of tapioca flour
- 1 ½ cups of brown rice flour
- 1 ½ cups of milk (at 110° F)
- 3 eggs

Directions:

- Check the manufacturer's instructions of your bread machine and add the ingredients to the bread pan accordingly. Usually, you would have to add the wet ingredients first then the dry ones.
- Choose the "gluten-free" setting on your bread maker if it has one. If not, choose the "basic" setting for baking white bread.
- Once cooked, take the bread pan out of your bread maker and allow it to rest for about 10 minutes before slicing.

Garlic Bread

This garlic bread goes perfectly with a plate of gluten-free pasta. However, you can also use it to make sandwiches with a unique taste. It's a savory recipe for your whole family to enjoy. When you toast it lightly, you can even top it off with avocado slices for a healthy, filling breakfast.

Nutritional Information: Approximately 167 calories per serving

Time: 2 hours and 20 minutes to 2 hours and 30 minutes

Servings Made: 12 servings

Prep Time: 10 minutes

Cook Time: 2 hours and 20 minutes to 2 hours and 30 minutes (This is an estimate based on average bread makers. Check your bread maker's instructions to confirm the proper time.)

Wet ingredients:

- 1 ½ tsp apple cider vinegar

BREAD MACHINE COOKBOOK

- 1 ½ tbsp maple syrup
- 2 tbsp butter (preferably vegan)
- 2 tbsp flax meal combined with 6 tbsp warm water (mix well then let stand for about 5 minutes)
- ⅛ cup of parsley (loosely chopped)
- ¾ cup of milk (dairy-free)
- 6 cloves of garlic (minced)

Dry ingredients:

- ½ tsp salt
- 1 tsp active dry yeast
- 1 ½ tsp xanthan gum
- 1 tbsp garlic powder
- 1 tbsp onion powder
- 2 tbsp potato starch
- ¼ cup of corn starch
- 1 ⅔ cups of brown rice flour

Directions:

- In a bowl, combine all the dry ingredients except for the yeast, then mix well.
- In the bread pan of your bread machine, add all of the wet ingredients then mix well.
- Add the mixture of dry ingredients on top of the wet ingredients.

BREAD MACHINE COOKBOOK

- Use your finger to make a well in the middle of the mound of dry ingredients.
- Add the dry yeast inside the well, making sure that it doesn't touch the wet mixture.
- Choose the "light crust" or "white bread" setting on your bread maker, then press the "start" button.
- Once cooked, take the bread pan out of your bread maker immediately so it doesn't burn.
- Allow the bread pan to cool down for about 10 minutes before slicing.

Multigrain Bread

This bread is soft, tender, and perfect for sandwiches. The grains give it a delicious flavor while the cornmeal provides a mild texture. When you toast slices of this bread, you will have crunchy, golden-brown pieces of bread.

Nutritional Information: Approximately 389 calories per serving

Time: 2 hours and 30 minutes to 2 hours and 40 minutes

Servings Made: 12

Prep Time: 10 minutes

Cook Time: 2 hours and 30 minutes to 2 hours and 40 minutes (This is an estimate based on average bread makers. Check your bread maker's instructions to confirm the proper time.)

Dry ingredients:

- 1 ¼ tsp sea salt
- 2 tsp xanthan gum

BREAD MACHINE COOKBOOK

- ⅓ cup of cornmeal (gluten-free)
- ½ cup of millet flour
- ⅔ cup of sorghum flour
- 1 cup of potato starch

Ingredients (for the yeast):

- 2 ¼ tsp instant dry yeast
- 1 ¼ cups of water (between 110 °F to 115°F)
- pinch of sugar

Wet ingredients:

- 1 tbsp caraway seeds
- 3 tbsp honey (you can also use raw agave nectar)
- 4 tbsp extra virgin olive oil
- ½ tsp rice vinegar (you can also use lemon juice)
- 2 large eggs (preferably organic, beaten)

Ingredients (grains):

- 1 tbsp sesame seeds (for topping)

Directions:

- Choose the "gluten-free" setting in your bread maker and choose either "dark" or "medium

BREAD MACHINE COOKBOOK

crust" according to your preference. You can also choose the "rapid rise" setting if your bread maker doesn't have a "gluten-free" setting.
- In a bowl, combine all of the dry ingredients, then mix well.
- In a separate bowl, combine the yeast ingredients and allow it to sit for about 5 minutes until it gets a bit foamy.
- Add all of the wet ingredients (along with the yeast mixture) in the bread pan of your bread maker then mix well.
- Pour the mixture of dry ingredients over the wet ingredients then close the lid of your bread maker.
- When the kneading or mixing cycle is done, open the lid of your bread maker and sprinkle sesame seeds on top of the bread.
- Close the lid and continue baking until the cycle finishes.
- Once cooked, take the bread pan out of your bread maker and place it on a wire rack to cool down. Test to see if it's done by giving it a tap. If it sounds hollow, it's done. If not, then you can continue baking it in your bread maker for about 5 to 10 more minutes. You

BREAD MACHINE COOKBOOK

can also continue baking it in the oven at 350°F for about 5 to 10 more minutes.

BREAD MACHINE COOKBOOK

Ciabatta Bread

Ciabatta is a type of Italian bread. It has a chewy texture and crumbly holes on the inside. This bread is perfect for making sandwiches and you can also toast it lightly with some butter for a yummy snack. Ciabatta is also the perfect bread to pair with soup. You can make this crusty bread in your bread maker for your whole family to enjoy.

Nutritional Information: Approximately 138 calories per serving

Time: 35 to 45 minutes

Servings Made: 12

Prep Time: 5 minutes

Cook Time: 30 to 40 minutes

Ingredients:

- ½ tsp salt
- 1 tsp sugar
- 1 ½ tsp active dry yeast
- 1 tbsp olive oil

BREAD MACHINE COOKBOOK

- 2 tbsp rosemary (dried)
- 1 ½ cup of water
- 3 ¼ cups of bread flour (gluten-free)

Directions:

- Check the manufacturer's instructions of your bread machine and add the ingredients to the bread pan accordingly. Usually, you would have to add the wet ingredients first then the dry ones.
- Choose the dough cycle of your bread maker, close the lid, and press the "start" button.
- Once the dough is formed, transfer it onto a clean, floured surface, cover the dough with plastic wrap, then allow to rest for about 20 minutes.
- Preheat your oven to 425°F and use parchment paper to line a baking sheet.
- Divide the ciabatta dough into 2 and form a loaf of bread with each portion.
- Place the loaves on the baking sheet and dust the top of each with flour.
- Spray some water over the loaves to make them crispy.
- Place the baking sheet in the oven and bake the ciabatta loaves for about 25 to 3o minutes.

BREAD MACHINE COOKBOOK

- Once baked, take the baking sheet out of the oven and allow the ciabatta loaves to cool down before slicing.

BREAD MACHINE COOKBOOK

Sourdough Bread

Although making sourdough bread is typically challenging, you can say goodbye to complex recipes as you let your bread maker do the work for you. As with the last recipe, you will be kneading the bread in your bread maker but you will finish off the task in the oven.

Nutritional Information: 126 calories per serving

Time: 4 hours and 55 minutes

Servings Made: 12

Prep Time: 4 hours and 10 minutes

Cook Time: 45 minutes

Ingredients:

- 1 ¾ tsp salt
- ½ tbsp sugar
- ¾ cup of fed sourdough starter
- 1 cup of water (lukewarm)
- 3 cups of bread flour
- cooking spray

BREAD MACHINE COOKBOOK

- cornmeal (for dusting)

Directions:

- In a bowl, combine all of the ingredients except the salt, and mix well.
- Form the dough into a bowl, cover with a damp towel, and then let it stand for about 1 to 2 hours.
- Place the dough ball in the bread pan of your bread maker and choose the dough cycle.
- Close the lid and press the "start" button.
- One the dough has been kneaded in your bread maker, take it out, and allow it to rise for about 2 to 3 hours.
- Line a baking sheet with parchment paper and sprinkle the surface with cornmeal.
- Shape the dough into an oval or round loaf then place it on the baking sheet. This type of dough is fairly sticky but it's not recommended to use flour while you're shaping it.
- Grease a sheet of plastic wrap with cooking spray and use it to cover the dough ball.
- Place the baking sheet in your refrigerator between 8 to 16 hours to proof.
- When you're ready to bake the bread, preheat your oven to 450°F.

BREAD MACHINE COOKBOOK

- Take the dough out of the oven, remove the plastic cover, and rub with gluten-free flour gently. Then slash the top of the loaf using a serrated knife.
- Place an empty baking sheet under the rack of your oven and pour a cup of water into it. This will create steam.
- Place the baking sheet with the dough on top of the rack then bake the sourdough bread for about 45 minutes.
- Once baked, take the baking sheet out of the oven and allow the sourdough bread to cool down for a minimum of 4 hours before you start slicing it.

BREAD MACHINE COOKBOOK

Olive and Onion Bread

This savory bread is better than the expensive artisan bread loaves you might find in your local bakery. All you need to make it are a few common ingredients and, of course, your bread maker. After baking it, you can enjoy this tasty, gluten-free bread with your family.

Nutritional Information: 199 calories per serving

Time: 2 hours and 20 minutes

Servings Made: 8

Prep Time: 10 minutes

Cook Time: 2 hours and 10 minutes

Ingredients:

- ¾ tsp thyme (dried)
- 1 tsp salt
- 2 tsp bread maker yeast
- 1 ½ tbsp white sugar (granulated)
- 2 tbsp olive oil
- ¼ cup of onion (dried, minced)

BREAD MACHINE COOKBOOK

- 1 cup of black olives (canned, chopped)
- 1 cup of water
- 2 cups of gluten-free flour blend

Directions:

- Add the water, olive oil, flour, sugar, salt, thyme, olives, onion, and yeast to the bread pan of your bread maker. Follow this order exactly.
- When you add the salt, sprinkle it away from the yeast. When you add the sugar, sprinkle it away from the yeast and at the opposite side of the salt. Also, create a well in the middle of the dry ingredients to sprinkle the yeast.
- Choose the "basic bread" setting in your bread maker, close the lid, and press the "start" button.
- Once cooked, take the bread pan out of the oven then allow the bread to cool down a bit before you start slicing.

Chapter 3: Making Sweet Bread Loaves

While the recipes shared in the previous chapter are perfect for making sandwiches, there are times when you just want to sink your teeth into something light and sweet. If your child is asking for a sweet snack or you are looking for something to satisfy your sweet tooth, these gluten-free recipes will hit the spot.

Pumpernickel Loaf

This recipe is simple and easy. It creates a lovely loaf of bread that you can share with your whole family. Once cooked, the loaf has enough moisture to be sliced thinly, and it's so soft and pliable that your children will surely keep asking you for more. You can bake this in your bread maker or you can also bake it in the oven... It's up to you!

BREAD MACHINE COOKBOOK

Nutritional Information: Approximately 141 calories per serving

Time: 1 hour and 40 minutes

Servings Made: 24 servings

Prep Time: 1 hour

Cook Time: 40 minutes

Ingredients:

- 1 tsp baking soda
- 1 ¼ tsp sea salt
- 2 ¼ tsp rapid rise yeast
- 1 tbsp cocoa powder (unsweetened)
- 3 tbsp apple cider vinegar
- 3 tbsp cane sugar (granulated; you can also use granulated unrefined sugar)
- 3 tbsp molasses (you can also use pure maple syrup)
- 3 tbsp olive oil
- ¼ cup of milk powder (not reconstituted, you can also use almond meal)
- ½ cup of apple cider (you can also use apple juice)
- ½ cup of yogurt (plain; you can also use water)

BREAD MACHINE COOKBOOK

- 1 cup of millet flour (gluten-free; you can also use gluten-free buckwheat flour)
- 2 cups of all-purpose flour (gluten-free)
- 2 eggs (whites only)
- 2 large eggs
- 2 tsp orange peel (optional; grated)
- 1 tbsp caraway seeds (optional)

Directions:

- In a bowl, add all of the wet ingredients. Make sure that they are at room temperature first.
- Whisk the ingredients together then pour the mixture into your bread maker's bread pan.
- In a separate bowl, add all of the dry ingredients except the yeast then mix well.
- Pour the mixture of dry ingredients over the wet ingredient mixture.
- Use your finger to make a well in the middle of the mound of dry ingredients.
- Add the dry yeast inside the well while making sure that it doesn't touch the wet mixture.
- Choose the "gluten-free" setting in your bread maker. Since the ingredients are for a 3-pound loaf of bread, choose the largest setting, too. Close the lid and press the "start" button.
- If your bread maker doesn't come with a gluten-free option, choose the "basic dough"

BREAD MACHINE COOKBOOK

setting. After your bread maker mixes the dough, choose the "bake" setting for 1 hour.
- You may have to adjust the cooking time as needed. You must only take the bread pan out of your bread maker if the internal temperature of the pumpernickel loaf is between 205°F to 210°F.
- Once cooked, take the bread pan out of the bread maker and allow it to cool for about 10 minutes before you remove the pumpernickel loaf to slice and serve.

Banana Pumpkin Loaf

This classic loaf of bread has been made gluten-free to suit your diet. It's great for breakfast or a sweet snack for your children. It has the same consistency as a cake, which makes this loaf tastier and more fun to eat.

Nutritional Information: Approximately 225 calories per serving

Time: 1 hour and 10 minutes to 1 hour and 30 minutes

Servings Made: 12

Prep Time: 10 minutes

Cook Time: 1 hour to 1 hour and 20 minutes

Ingredients:

- ½ tsp of salt
- 1 tsp of baking powder
- 3 tbsp maple syrup
- ½ cup of butter (softened)
- ½ cup of sugar

BREAD MACHINE COOKBOOK

- 2 cups of all-purpose flour (gluten-free)
- 2 eggs
- 3 bananas (very ripe, mashed)

Directions:

- In a bowl, add all of the ingredients then mix well
- Pour the mixture into the bread pan of your bread maker.
- Choose the "cake" setting on your bread maker.
- Close the lid and push the "start" button.
- Once cooked, take the bread pan out of your bread maker and allow it to rest for about 10 minutes before removing to slice and serve.

BREAD MACHINE COOKBOOK

Honey Oat Loaf

This bread loaf has just the right amount of sweetness; it's also soft and super moist. Since honey is a healthy ingredient, it makes this loaf healthier and yummier. Serve a few slices to your child with a glass of milk for a sweet and filling snack.

Nutritional Information: Approximately 265 calories per serving

Time: 2 hours and 30 minutes to 2 hours and 40 minutes

Servings Made: 12

Prep Time: 10 minutes

Cook Time: 2 hours and 30 minutes to 2 hours and 40 minutes (This is an estimate based on average bread makers. Check your bread maker's instructions to confirm the proper time.)

Ingredients:

- ¾ tsp salt
- 1 ½ tsp sugar

BREAD MACHINE COOKBOOK

- 2 tsp xanthan gum
- 1 ½ tbsp yeast
- 3 tbsp butter (melted)
- 3 tbsp honey
- ½ cup of potato starch
- 1 ¼ cups of brown rice flour
- 1 ¼ cups of oats (gluten-free)
- 1 ¼ cups of water (warm)
- 2 eggs

Directions:

- Check the manufacturer's instructions of your bread machine and add the ingredients to the bread pan accordingly. Usually, you would have to add the wet ingredients first then the dry ones.
- Choose the "gluten-free" setting of your bread maker, close the lid, and press the "start" button.
- Once cooked, take the bread pan out of your bread maker and allow the loaf to cool down for about 15 minutes before removing to slice and serve.

BREAD MACHINE COOKBOOK

Cinnamon Loaf with Raisins

Just because you have started your kids on a gluten-free diet, that doesn't mean that you should only serve them boring loaves of bread. This recipe is sweet, tasty, and healthy too. It's a gluten-free twist on the classic cinnamon loaf recipe that your kids will surely love.

Nutritional Information: Approximately 233 calories per serving

Time: 2 hours and 20 minutes to 2 hours and 30 minutes

Servings Made: 12

Prep Time: 5 minutes

Cook Time: 2 hours and 15 minutes to 2 hours and 25 minutes (This is an estimate based on average bread makers. Check your bread maker's instructions to confirm the proper time.)

Ingredients:

- 1 tsp apple cider vinegar

BREAD MACHINE COOKBOOK

- 1 tsp cinnamon (ground)
- 1 tsp sea salt
- 1 tbsp active dry yeast
- 1 tbsp xanthan gum
- 3 tbsp butter (unsalted; melted)
- 3 eggs
- ¼ cup of honey
- ⅓ cup of raisins
- ½ cup of brown flaxseed meal (preferably organic)
- ½ cup of Mighty Tasty Hot Cereal (gluten-free)
- 1 ¼ cups of milk
- 2 cups of brown rice flour

Directions:

- Before you start combining the ingredients, make sure that they are all at room temperature.
- Check the manufacturer's instructions of your bread machine and add the ingredients to the bread pan accordingly.
- Choose the "basic white bread" setting on your bread maker. Close the lid and press the "start" button.
- Once cooked, take the bread pan out of your bread maker then allow it to cool down for

BREAD MACHINE COOKBOOK

about 10 minutes or so before you start slicing.

Pull-Apart Lemony Bread

This sweet bread isn't technically a loaf but it's sweet enough to fall into the category. With this recipe, you'll need a bundt pan along with your bread maker. It's citrusy, sweet, and oh-so-addictive!

Nutritional Information: Approximately 467 calories per serving

Time: 4 hours and 15 minutes

Serving Made: 8

Prep Time: 3 hours and 45 minutes

Cook Time: 30 minutes

Ingredients:

- 1 tsp salt
- 2 ¼ tsp bread machine yeast
- 2 tbsp whipping cream (you can also use milk)
- ¼ cup of butter (for the dough)
- ¼ cup of butter (melted; for the coating)
- ¼ cup of sugar
- ⅝ cup of milk

BREAD MACHINE COOKBOOK

- 1 cup of sugar (powdered)
- 3 ¼ cups of flour (unbleached; gluten-free)
- 2 eggs
- lemon zest (taken from 3 lemons and 1 orange combined with ½ cup of sugar)

Directions:

- In the bread pan of your bread maker, add the milk, sugar, salt, butter, eggs, flour, and yeast, then mix well.
- Choose the dough cycle, close the lid, and press the "start" button.
- After about 5 minutes, open the lid to check the dough. If you see that it's too wet, add a tablespoon of flour. If it's too dry, add a tablespoon of milk. Keep adding until you get the right consistency.
- Close the lid and allow the dough cycle to finish until the dough doubles in size.
- Transfer the dough to a clean surface that has been sprinkled with flour, and use a rolling pin to roll the dough into a rectangle.
- Use a knife to cut out big "diamonds" from the dough.
- Dip the dough into the butter, and then coat it with the citrus zest mixture.

BREAD MACHINE COOKBOOK

- Place one "diamond" into the bundt pan on its side. Place the second diamond against the first one, making sure it's upright. Continue adding "diamonds" until the entire bundt pan has been covered. If needed, squeeze the last "diamonds" together.
- Cover the bundt pan with plastic wrap and let sit somewhere warm until the size of the dough doubles.
- Uncover the bundt pan, then place it in your oven which you have preheated to 350°F.
- Bake the bread for about 30 to 35 minutes until it reaches an internal temperature of 190°F.
- Once cooked, take the bundt pan out of the oven then allow it to cool for about 5 minutes or so before turning the bundt pan over and removing the bread.
- In a bowl, add the powdered sugar with whipping cream then mix well.
- Drizzle the mixture over the lemon bread while warm, and then serve.

BREAD MACHINE COOKBOOK

Making Recipes Gluten-Free

Gluten is very common in baked goods because it provides structure to bread and pastries. Without gluten, cakes collapse, bread comes out hard, and cookies crumble. Fortunately, there are many gluten-free ingredients available that you can use as alternatives to make virtually any recipe gluten-free. The most common ingredients to include in your gluten-free baking are eggs, to add protein to the recipe, and xanthan gum, which acts as a stabilizer, thickener, and emulsifier. This is why you may have noticed that all of the recipes shared here contain either one or both of these essential ingredients. Essentially, these ingredients provide structure to your gluten-free baked goods. Here are some tips that will help you become a gluten-free baking and cooking master:

- **For Baking Bread**

    For most types of bread, you can replace the flour with gluten-free flour. Just make sure that the recipe also has some type of stabilizing ingredient like cream cheese, yogurt, sour cream, and the like to keep the bread moist. Alternatively, you can also look for recipes online that are specifically gluten-free. This is the better option if you're not sure how to make substitutions.

- **For Baking Pastries**

The simplest way to make pastry recipes gluten-free is by using a 1:1 ratio of gluten-free flour. Then make sure to use a binding agent like guar gum or xanthan gum. This is especially important for cakes, muffins, cookies, and other baked pastries. Generally, you must add 1 teaspoon of the binding agent for each cup of gluten-free flour.

- **For Cooking Pasta**

If you want to make gluten-free pasta dishes, the simplest thing you can do is replace the pasta with gluten-free options. You don't have to avoid pasta, as there are many options for gluten-free pasta available these days. Just make sure to read the instructions on the packaging so you don't end up overcooking the noodles. Also, choose gluten-free sauce recipes to make sure that the whole dish doesn't contain any gluten.

BREAD MACHINE COOKBOOK

- **For Cooking Sauces or Soup**

When cooking soups or sauces, use arrowroot powder, potato starch, or gluten-free cornstarch to thicken your dish as a substitute for flour. When replacing flour in the recipe, only use half the quantity needed. For instance, if the recipe calls for ½ cup of flour, replace this with ¼ cup of arrowroot powder, potato starch, or gluten-free cornstarch.

- **For a Gluten-Free Flour Mixture**

Although you can already find different types of gluten-free flour in stores, you can also create your own flour mixture that's completely free of gluten. For this, combine the following ingredients:

- 1 teaspoon xanthan gum for every 1 ½ cups of the gluten-free flour mixture
- 1 part of tapioca starch or tapioca flour
- 2 parts of potato starch
- 3 parts of brown or white rice flour

When it comes to baking and cooking gluten-free dishes, you may want to experiment with different

BREAD MACHINE COOKBOOK

ingredients. If you want to learn how to cook different kinds of dishes, do your research. Also, a little bit of trial-and-error goes a long way. Just have fun discovering what works and what doesn't. Keep trying until you become a true gluten-free master chef!

Chapter 4: Getting Creative with Pastries

If you have a bread maker at home, you don't have to limit yourself to making different kinds of bread on it. The great thing about bread makers is that they are very versatile. You can even use them to make different types of pastries. Whether you need to use your bread maker to create the dough or bake the pastries all the way to the end, you will discover that this clever little kitchen appliance is a lot more useful than it looks!

Bagels

While you can easily buy gluten-free bagels from bakeries and food shops, it's much more satisfying to serve homemade bagels to your children. If you make bagels at home, you can be sure that they are healthy, tasty, and only contain gluten-free ingredients. These

BREAD MACHINE COOKBOOK

bagels are chewy, soft, and a lot better than any bagels you can buy from stores.

Nutritional Information: 74 calories per serving

Time: 1 hour and 40 minutes to 1 hour and 50 minutes

Servings Made: 8 bagels

Prep Time: 20 minutes

Cook Time: 1 hour and 20 minutes to 1 hour and 30 minutes

Ingredients:

- 1 ½ tsp salt
- 2 tsp active dry yeast
- 1 ½ tbsp sugar (granulated)
- 1 ¼ cups of water (warm)
- 3 ½ cups of all-purpose flour (gluten-free)
- egg wash mixture (1 egg and 1 tbsp of water beaten together)
- Your choice of toppings like sesame seeds, poppy seeds, coarse salt, shredded cheese, and more

Directions:

BREAD MACHINE COOKBOOK

- In the bread pan of your bread machine, add the water, flour, sugar, and salt. Follow this order of ingredients.
- Use your finger to make a well in the middle of the dry ingredients.
- Add the dry yeast inside the well, then cover it with the flour.
- Choose the "dough" setting on your bread maker, close the lid, and press the "start" button.
- When the dough has been formed, punch it down into the pan then allow it to rest for about 10 minutes.
- Take the dough out of the bread pan, and then divide it into eight portions. If you want to make smaller bagels, divide the dough into more portions.
- Roll each portion of dough into a ball.
- Coat your hands with gluten-free flour and gently shape the dough balls into rings to form bagels.
- Place the bagels on a clean, floured surface, and use a damp kitchen towel to cover them up. Allow the bagels to rest for about 10 minutes.
- Preheat your oven to 425°F as you line a baking sheet with parchment paper.

BREAD MACHINE COOKBOOK

- Add water to a pot and bring to a boil.
- Use a slotted spoon to add the bagels into the pot. You can add 2 to 3 bagels at a time depending on the size of your pot.
- Cook the bagels for about 1 to 2 minutes, flip them over, and continue cooking for about 1 to 2 minutes more. The longer you cook the bagels, the chewier they will be.
- Transfer the bagels to the baking sheet you have prepared and brush with the egg wash mixture.
- If desired, sprinkle each bagel with your choice of toppings.
- Place the baking sheet in the oven and bake the bagels for about 20 minutes.
- Once cooked, take the baking sheet out of the oven then allow the bagels to cool down before serving.

BREAD MACHINE COOKBOOK

Chocolate Chip Brioche

Doesn't this pastry sound fancy? Brioche is a type of French bread that's enriched with milk, eggs, and sugar. It's richer, sweeter, and softer than other types of bread. Fortunately, you can also make brioche sans the gluten. All you need is a recipe just like this one to make your own brioche at home for your kids to enjoy.

Nutritional Information: 146 calories per serving

Time: 2 hours and 30 minutes

Servings Made: 18 brioche rolls

Prep Time: 30 minutes

Cook Time: 15 minutes

Ingredients for the brioche:

- 1 ½ tsp instant yeast
- 1 ½ tsp salt
- 3 tbsp sugar
- 4 tbsp butter (unsalted)
- ½ cup of milk

BREAD MACHINE COOKBOOK

- ½ cup of water
- 1 ½ cups chocolate chips
- 3 ¾ cups of all-purpose flour (gluten-free; more if needed)
- 3 eggs
- cooking spray

Ingredients for the topping:

- 1 egg (beaten)
- pearl sugar or sparkling sugar

Directions:

- In a microwave-safe bowl, add the milk, butter, and water.
- Place the bowl in the microwave then heat on low for about 45 to 60 seconds.
- In the bread pan of your bread maker, add all of the ingredients except for the chocolate chips.
- Choose the "dough" setting on your bread maker, close the lid, and press the "start" button.
- When there are only 3 minutes or so left in the kneading cycle of your bread maker, open the lid and add the chocolate chips.
- Close the lid and wait until the cycle finishes.

BREAD MACHINE COOKBOOK

- Once kneaded completely, transfer the dough to a lightly-greased bowl, cover it, and let it sit for about 1 hour until the dough doubles in size.
- Transfer the dough to a clean surface dusted with gluten-free flour.
- Divide the dough into eighteen portions, and then roll each portion into balls.
- Line a baking sheet with parchment paper and place the brioche rolls on it.
- Brush the top of each brioche roll with egg then sprinkle with sugar.
- Cover the baking sheet with plastic wrap that you have greased with cooking spray. Set aside for about 45 minutes.
- About 5 to 10 minutes before baking, preheat your oven to 400°F.
- Remove the plastic wrap from the baking sheet and place it in the oven.
- Bake the brioche rolls for about 15 to 17 minutes.
- Once cooked, take the baking sheet out of the oven and allow it to cool down slightly before serving. These are best served while still a bit warm.

Soft Pretzels

With a bread maker at home, making soft pretzels at home is a breeze. This recipe allows you to make chewy, soft, and gluten-free pretzels just like the ones you can buy from street vendors. These soft and buttery pretzels are the perfect snack. When you pair them with sweet or savory dips, your children will surely beg you to make more.

Nutritional Information: 291 calories per serving

Time: 2 hours and 7 minutes

Servings Made: 6 pretzels

Prep Time: 1 hour and 55 minutes

Cook Time: 12 minutes

Ingredients:

- 1 tsp salt
- 2 tsp coarse salt (for topping)
- 2 tsp dry active yeast
- 1 tbsp butter (at room temperature)
- 2 tbsp sugar

BREAD MACHINE COOKBOOK

- 3 tbsp butter (melted)
- ⅓ cup of baking soda (for cooking)
- 1 cup of water (at room temperature)
- 2 ¾ cups of all-purpose flour (gluten-free)
- 1 egg
- 6 cups of water (for cooking)
- egg wash mixture (1 egg and 1 tbsp of water beaten together)

Directions:

- In the bread pan of your bread maker, add 1 cup of water, butter, sugar, salt, flour, and yeast. Follow this order of ingredients but don't mix.
- Choose the "dough" setting on your bread maker, close the lid, and press the "start" button.
- Once the dough has formed, transfer it to a clean surface dusted with gluten-free flour.
- Before you continue, preheat your oven to 400°F and use parchment paper to line a baking sheet.
- Divide the dough into 6 portions then roll each portion into a long dough rope.
- Gently twist the dough rope to form a pretzel and press down on the parts where the dough intersects to maintain the shape.

BREAD MACHINE COOKBOOK

- In a pot, add 6 cups of water over medium heat and bring to a rapid simmer.
- Add the baking soda gradually while stirring to dissolve the powder.
- Turn the heat down to low.
- Use a slotted spoon to add the pretzels into the pot. You can add 1 to 2 pretzels depending on the size of your pot.
- Cook the pretzels for about 30 seconds, flip them over, and then continue cooking for 30 seconds more.
- Once cooked, transfer the pretzels to the baking sheet that you have prepared.
- Brush each of the pretzels with the egg wash then sprinkle with salt.
- Place the baking sheet in the oven and bake the pretzels for about 10 to 12 minutes.
- Once cooked, take the baking sheet out of the oven and brush each of the pretzels with melted butter.
- Allow the pretzels to cool down slightly before serving. These are best served while still a bit warm.

Challah

Whether you're Jewish or not, this tasty bread will be an interesting addition to your child's diet. This special bread is traditionally eaten on ceremonial Jewish occasions and holidays. You can braid it to look like the traditional bread but you can also prepare it like a "normal" loaf of bread. It's totally up to you!

Nutritional Information: 123 calories per serving

Time: 1 hour and 45 minutes

Servings Made: 16

Prep Time: 60 minutes

Cook Time: 45 minutes

Ingredients:

- 1 ¼ tsp yeast
- 1 ½ tsp salt
- 2 ½ tbsp vegetable oil (vegetable)
- ½ cup of honey
- 1 cup of water (lukewarm)

BREAD MACHINE COOKBOOK

- 4 ⅔ cups of bread flour (gluten-free)
- 1 large egg (lightly beaten)
- 1 large egg (yolk only, lightly beaten)
- egg wash mixture (1 egg and 1 tbsp of water beaten together)
- poppy seeds or sesame seeds (optional, for topping)

Directions:

- In the bread pan of your bread maker, add the salt, egg, egg yolk, water, honey, and oil.
- Gently spoon the flour over the liquid ingredients.
- Use your finger to make a well in the middle of the dry ingredients.
- Add the dry yeast inside the well then cover it with the flour.
- Choose the "white", "basic", or "sweet" setting of your bread maker, close the lid, and press the "start" button.
- When the final rise cycle of your bread maker starts, press the "pause" button.
- Transfer the dough on a clean surface dusted with gluten-free flour.
- Punch the dough down gently then divide it into 3 portions. Roll each of the portions into a long dough rope.

BREAD MACHINE COOKBOOK

- Arrange the dough ropes side by side and braid them snugly. Tuck the ends underneath to create an oval-shaped loaf of bread.
- Brush the top of the braided loaf with the egg wash and top with seeds if desired.
- Take out the kneading paddles from your bread pan and place the loaf back in it.
- Close the lid, press the "start" button, and wait until it is finished.
- Once cooked, take the bread pan out and allow to cool before you remove the challah loaf for slicing and serving.

Donuts

Most kids love donuts and with this recipe, you can allow them to have this classic snack without worrying about gluten. These donuts are fluffy, light, and they go perfectly with different kinds of topping. After baking them, you can even ask your children to customize their own donuts by adding their favorite toppings. Wouldn't that be a lot of fun?

Nutritional Information: 189 calories per serving

Time: 2 hours and 3 minutes

Servings Made: 12 donuts

Prep Time: 2 hours

Cook Time: 3 minutes

Ingredients:

- 1 tsp salt
- 2 ½ tsp bread machine yeast
- ¼ cup butter (softened, at room temperature)
- ¼ cup of sugar (granulated)
- ¼ cup of water (at room temperature)

BREAD MACHINE COOKBOOK

- ⅔ cup of milk (slightly warmed)
- 3 cups of bread flour (gluten-free)
- 4 cups of oil (for deep frying)
- 1 egg (lightly beaten)
- ¼ cup of confectioner's sugar (optional, for topping)

Directions:

- In the bread pan of your bread maker, add milk, water, butter, egg, sugar, salt, flour, and yeast. Follow this order of ingredients but don't mix.
- Choose the "dough" setting on your bread maker, close the lid, and push the "start" button.
- Once finished, transfer the dough to a clean surface dusted with gluten-free flour.
- Use a rolling pin to roll the dough until it's about ½ inch thick.
- Use a donut cutter to cut out the donut shapes. You can also use a circle-shaped cookie cutter for this step.
- Use wax paper to line a baking sheet and place the donuts on it.
- Cover the donuts with another sheet of wax paper and top with a clean tea towel.

BREAD MACHINE COOKBOOK

- Allow the donuts to rise for about 30 to 40 minutes.
- When you're ready to cook, add the oil to a pot and heat to 375°F. You can also use a deep fryer.
- Add the donuts and fry for about 3 minutes each. You can fry 2 to 3 donuts at a time.
- Once cooked, transfer the donuts to a plate lined with a paper towel to drain any excess oil.
- While hot, sprinkle the top of each donut with sugar or your child's favorite toppings.
- Allow the donuts to cool down slightly before serving.

Chapter 5: Surprising Things You Can Cook in Your Bread Maker

Did you know that you can make more than just bread, pastries, and other baked goods in your bread machine? It's true! In this chapter, we will go through some simple non-bread recipes that you can easily make for your kids. These recipes are simple, healthy, tasty, and gluten-free. After you have practiced making different recipes in your bread maker, you can start experimenting to come up with your own creative dishes!

Meatloaf

Yes, you can make meatloaf in your bread maker too. Your simple kitchen appliance is so incredibly versatile that you can make entire meals in it. Since the original recipe called for bread crumbs, a simple substitution made it gluten-free to suit your diet.

Nutritional Information: Approximately 164 calories per serving

Time: 1 hour and 20 minutes

Servings Made: 8

Prep Time: 10 minutes

Cook Time: 1 hour and 10 minutes

Ingredients for the meatloaf:

- ¼ tsp black pepper
- 1 tsp garlic powder
- 2 tsp salt
- 2 tbsp parsley (fresh and chopped)
- 1 cup of mushrooms (sliced)
- 1 cup of pork rinds (crushed finely)
- 2 lbs sirloin (ground)
- 1 onion (chopped)
- 2 large eggs (lightly beaten)

Ingredients for the glaze:

- 1 tsp mustard
- 1 tbsp brown sugar

BREAD MACHINE COOKBOOK

- ½ cup of ketchup (you can also use barbecue sauce)

Directions:

- In a bowl, combine all of the ingredients and mix well.
- In a separate bowl, combine the glaze ingredients, mix well, and then set aside.
- Take out the kneading blades of your bread maker's bread pan then press the meat mixture into the pan.
- Choose the "bake" setting of your bread maker but turn off the "preheat", "knead", and "rise" cycles. Close the lid and push the "start" button.
- When there are only 30 minutes left on the timer, open the lid of your bread maker then pour the glaze over the meatloaf.
- Close your bread maker's lid and allow the cycle to finish.
- Once cooked, take the bread pan out of your bread maker. Allow the meatloaf to cool down a bit then drain the juices, remove from the pan, and start slicing.

BREAD MACHINE COOKBOOK

Fresh Fruit Jams

Aside from making healthy, gluten-free bread, you can also make fresh fruit jams in your bread maker. Here is a simple recipe to do this plus a couple of options for making different types of jam.

Nutritional Information: Approximately 49 calories per serving (around 2 tablespoons of jam)

Time: 1 hour and 35 minutes to 1 hour and 45 minutes

Servings Made: 1 jar

Prep Time: 35 minutes

Cook Time: 1 hour to 1 hour and 10 minutes

Ingredients for blueberry jam:

- 2 ½ cups of sugar (granulated)
- 5 cups of blueberries (frozen or fres;, you can also use a combination of these)
- 1 tbsp no-sugar pectin (optional)

Directions:

BREAD MACHINE COOKBOOK

- Add blueberries to a food processor and pulse to mash.
- Add the sugar and the pectin (if using) to the mashed blueberries and mix well.
- Pour the blueberry mixture into your bread maker's bread pan.
- Choose the "jelly" or "jam" cycle, close the lid, and push the "start" button.
- Once done, open the lid, and allow the jam to cool for about 30 minutes before transferring to a jar or any other airtight container.
- Allow to rest for about 3 hours or so before serving. You can store it in your refrigerator for up to 1 month.

You can follow these directions for other jams and jellies by changing the ingredients but following the same steps. For example, to make apricot jam, you would add apricots you've properly prepared (peeled, pitted, and cut) to a food processor and pulse to mash.

Ingredients for apricot jam:

- 2 cups of apricots (ripe but firm, peeled, pitted, cut in half)
- 2 cups of sugar (granulated)
- 1 tbsp no-sugar pectin (optional)

BREAD MACHINE COOKBOOK

Ingredients for blackberry jam:

- 2 ½ cups of sugar (granulated)
- 5 cups of blackberries
- 1 tbsp no-sugar pectin (optional)

Ingredients for crabapple jelly:

- 2 cups of sugar
- 4 cups of crabapple juice
- 2 packs of gelatin

Ingredients for grape jelly:

- 1 tbsp lemon juice
- 1 cup of sugar
- 2 cups of grape juice
- 2 packs of gelatin

Ingredients for mulberry jam:

- 2 cups sugar (granulated)
- 4 cups of mulberries
- 2 packs of gelatin

Ingredients peach jam:

- 2 cups of sugar (granulated)

BREAD MACHINE COOKBOOK

- 4 cups of peaches (ripe, peeled, pitted, cut in half; you can also use canned or frozen peaches)
- 1 tbsp no-sugar pectin (optional)

Ingredients for raspberry jam:

- 2 cups of sugar (granulated)
- 4 cups of raspberries (fresh)
- 1 tbsp no-sugar pectin (optional)

Ingredients for strawberry jam:

- 3 cups of sugar (granulated)
- 8 cups of strawberries (fresh)
- 1 tbsp no-sugar pectin (optional)

Butternut Squash Soup

Having a warm bowl of hearty soup on a chilly day is amazing. If your children are fans of thick soups, you will be delighted to know that you can also make soup in your bread maker. Pair this soup with a slice of freshly-baked bread for a healthy, filling meal.

Nutritional Information: Approximately 401 calories per serving

Time: 1 hour and 40 minutes

Servings Made: 3 bowls

Prep Time: 10 minutes

Cook Time: 1 hour and 30 minutes

Ingredients:

- 1 tsp cumin (ground)
- 2 tsp Chinese Five-Spice powder
- 4 tbsp coconut cream
- ¼ cup of root ginger (finely chopped)
- 2 ½ cups of vegetable stock
- 1 onion (chopped)

BREAD MACHINE COOKBOOK

- 1 small butternut squash (cubed)
- 2 green chilies
- 2 limes (juiced)
- 2 sticks of lemongrass (the soft parts in the middle)
- black pepper
- salt

Directions:

- Add all of the ingredients into the bread pan of your bread maker.
- Choose the "jam" setting then set the timer to 1 hour and 30 minutes.
- Close the lid of your bread maker and push the "start" button.
- Once cooked, pour the mixture into a blender.
- Blend until you get a smooth texture then transfer the soup to serving bowls.

Mushroom and Cranberry Risotto

This dish might sound fancy but it's actually very easy to make—especially when you have a bread maker at home. This recipe is a unique approach to cooking risotto and the results will amaze you.

Nutrition Information: Approximately 638 calories per serving

Time: 55 minutes

Servings Made: 3

Prep Time: 15 minutes

Cook Time: 40 minutes

Ingredients:

- ½ tsp of olive oil
- 1 ½ tsp rosemary (fresh, chopped)
- 1 tbsp garlic (minced)
- ⅓ cup of cranberries (frozen)
- 1 cup of mushrooms (sliced)
- 1 cup of rice
- 2 ½ cups of vegetable stock

BREAD MACHINE COOKBOOK

Directions:

- In a pan, add the olive oil over medium-high heat.
- Add the garlic and mushrooms to the pan. Roast for about 3 to 4 minutes.
- In a bowl, add the cranberries and mash them.
- Add all of the ingredients into the bread pan of your bread maker.
- Choose the "jam" setting and set the timer to 40 minutes. Close the lid and press the "start" button. You can continue cooking for about 5 to 10 minutes more if the risotto isn't cooked yet.
- Once cooked, transfer the risotto to serving plates and serve while hot.

Peach Cobbler

Cobbler is the ultimate dessert but it also serves as an amazingly tasty snack. You can make this dish using the freshest fruits of the season, but using frozen peaches works well too. This is the bread maker dish for you to make and practice on before you start experimenting with your own ingredients and recipes.

Nutritional Information: Approximately 342 calories per serving

Time: 1 hour and 25 minutes

Servings Made: 6

Prep Time: 15 minutes

Cook Time: 1 hour and 10 minutes

Ingredients for the peach filling:

- ⅛ tsp salt
- 1 tsp vanilla extract
- 2 tbsp lemon juice (freshly squeezed)
- ¼ cup of pie filling enhancer
- ⅔ cup of sugar

BREAD MACHINE COOKBOOK

- 6 peaches (ripe, peeled, pitted, sliced; you can also use 4 heaping cups of frozen peaches, sliced)

Ingredients for the cobbler:

- ¼ tsp salt
- 1 ½ tsp baking powder
- 3 tbsp sugar
- 4 tbsp butter (cold; cut into pieces)
- ½ cup of milk (you can also use cream)
- 1 ½ cups of all-purpose flour (gluten-free)
- Cooking spray

Directions:

- In a bowl, combine all of the peach filling ingredients, and mix well.
- Spoon the peach filling mixture into the bread pan.
- In a separate bowl, combine the sugar, baking powder, salt, and flour then whisk well.
- Use your finger to work the pieces of butter into the mixture until you get a crumbly texture.
- Pour the milk into the mixture and stir until combined.

BREAD MACHINE COOKBOOK

- Add the cobbler mixture over the peach filling in a single layer.
- Take out the paddles from your bread maker then use cooking spray to grease the bread pan lightly.
- Choose the "bake" setting of your bread maker then set the timer to 70 minutes.
- Close the lid of your bread maker and press the "start" button.
- Once cooked, open the lid and serve the cobbler immediately. You can also activate the "keep-warm" setting of your bread maker and serve when ready.

Conclusion: Let's Get Cooking!

There you have it!

Now you have the fundamental information you need to know about your bread maker along with many gluten-free recipes to start cooking for your children. Use this knowledge to make the most out of this clever kitchen appliance. Brush the dust off your bread maker and discover all the settings and functions it has. That way, you can determine which dishes you can make and which ones you might have to modify because of the limitations of your appliance.

You can use the versatility of bread makers to have interesting new cooking experiences. When you have tried making all of these recipes, you can go online and look for more. You also have the option to purchase another awesome gluten-free bread maker cookbook (like this one!) to learn how to make other types of bread, pastries, and dishes using your bread maker. Amaze your children and the rest of your family with these recipes, and don't forget to have fun while you're at it! With a bread maker in your kitchen, cooking has never been this simple.

BREAD MACHINE COOKBOOK

Bluesource And Friends

This book is brought to you by Bluesource And Friends, a happy book publishing company.

Our motto is **"Happiness Within Pages"**

We promise to deliver amazing value to readers with our books.

We also appreciate honest book reviews from our readers.

Connect with us on our Facebook page www.facebook.com/bluesourceandfriends and stay tuned to our latest book promotions and free giveaways.

References

Allrich, K. (2009, March 21). Gluten-Free Multi-Grain Sandwich Bread. *Gluten Free Goddess Recipes*. https://glutenfreegoddess.blogspot.com/2009/03/gluten-free-multi-grain-sandwich-bread.html

Atkinson, A. (n.d.). Gluten-Free White Bread for Bread Machines. *All Recipes*. https://www.allrecipes.com/recipe/7185/gluten-free-white-bread-for-bread-machines/

Bob's Red Mill. (2020). *GF Cinnamon Raisin Bread for the Bread Machine*. https://www.bobsredmill.com/recipes/how-to-make/gf-cinnamon-raisin-bread-for-the-bread-machine/

Bread Dad. (n.d.). *List of Bread Machine Benefits*. https://breaddad.com/bread-machine-benefits/

Bucklin, S. (2018, October 29). *Who Really Should Be on a Gluten-Free Diet?* Everyday Health. https://www.everydayhealth.com/digestive-health/who-really-should-be-on-a-gluten-free-diet.aspx

Carver, C. (2020, April 30). Easy Gluten-Free Bread Recipe For an Oven or Bread Machine. *Gluten-Free Palate*. https://www.glutenfreepalate.com/gluten-free-bread-recipe/

Chan, K. (2011, November 12). Gluten Free Oat & Honey Bread. *Gluten-Free Gobsmacked*. http://www.glutenfreegobsmacked.com/2011/11/gluten-free-oat-honey-bread/

Forrest, C. (2020, May 8). 6 Reasons to Go Gluten Free (Even If You're Not Celiac). *Clean Eating Kitchen*. https://www.cleaneatingkitchen.com/why-go-gluten-free-non-celiac/

BREAD MACHINE COOKBOOK

Gilson, T. (2018, March 24). Bread Machine Onion & Olive Bread. *Food Meanderings.* https://foodmeanderings.com/bread-machine-bread-onion-olive/

Hamel, P. (2015, February 20). Making a recipe gluten-free. *King Arthur Flour.* https://www.kingarthurflour.com/blog/2015/02/20/making-recipe-gluten-free

Katie. (2019, October 21). Simple Bread Machine Sourdough. *Heart's Content Farmhouse.* https://heartscontentfarmhouse.com/bread-machine-sourdough/

King, G. (2018, January 21). Easy Bread Machine Donuts. *Art and the Kitchen.* https://www.artandthekitchen.com/easy-bread-machine-donuts/

King, L. (2019, January 27). Bread Machine Pretzels. *Art and the Kitchen.* https://www.artandthekitchen.com/bread-machine-pretzels/

King Arthur Flour. (n.d.). *Peach Cobbler à la Bread Machine.* https://www.kingarthurflour.com/recipes/peach-cobbler-a-la-bread-machine-recipe

Kuzemchak, S. (2017, August 15). How to Make Bagels With Your Bread Machine. *Real Mom Nutrition.* https://www.realmomnutrition.com/bread-machine-bagels/

Levy, G. (2020, June 1). 14 Bread Machine Tips. *Backdoor Survival.* https://www.backdoorsurvival.com/14-tips-for-bread-machine-users/

Lewis, S. & Strealy, N. (2019). *Three Reasons To Go Gluten Free and Three Reasons Not To.* Providence Health & Services. https://oregon.providence.org/forms-and-information/t/three-reasons-to-go-gluten-free-and-three-reasons-not-to/

Martin, A. (2015, May 16). How to Make Almost Any Recipe Gluten Free. *Blessed Beyond Crazy.* https://blessedbeyondcrazy.com/how-to-make-almost-any-recipe-gluten-free/

Nubie, S. (2016, October 11). Jellies and Jams Recipes from Your Bread Machine. *Bread Maker Machines.*

BREAD MACHINE COOKBOOK

https://www.breadmakermachines.com/jellies-and-jams-bread-machine/

Nubie, S. (2017, July 30). 100% Buckwheat Bread (Gluten Free) Recipe. *Bread Maker Machines.* https://www.breadmakermachines.com/recipes/100-buckwheat-bread-gluten-free-recipe/

Nubie, S. (2017, December 18). Gluten Free Banana Bread Recipe. *Bread Maker Machines.* https://www.breadmakermachines.com/recipes/gluten-free-banana-bread-recipe/

Reed, P. (2018, June 12). Easy Ciabatta Bread. *Brooklyn Farm Girl.* https://brooklynfarmgirl.com/easy-ciabatta-bread/

Rhodes, P. (2013, December 14). Lemon Pull-Apart Bread Made Simple With a Bread Machine. *Salad in a Jar.* https://saladinajar.com/recipes/lemony-pull-apart-bread-made-simple-with-a-bread-machine-and-a-bundt-pan/

Rhodes, P. (2017, May 5). Cranberry and Mushroom Risotto. *Cape Cod Select.* https://www.capecodselect.com/recipes/cranberry-and-mushroom-risotto/

River, W. (2016, October 18). *Top 7 Advantages of a Bread Maker Over Traditional Methods.* White River Kitchens. https://www.whiteriverkitchens.co.uk/top-advantages-of-a-bread-maker/

Rolek, B. (2019, June 19). Jewish Bread Machine Challah. *The Spruce Eats.* https://www.thespruceeats.com/jewish-bread-machine-challah-recipe-1135939

Salaky, K. (2020, May 5). So You Bought A Bread Maker? Here's How To Put It To Good Use. *Delish.* https://www.delish.com/kitchen-tools/cookware-reviews/a32337661/how-to-use-bread-maker-machine/

Shaw, K. (2020, February 3). Chocolate Chip Brioche. *Heart's Content Farmhouse.* https://heartscontentfarmhouse.com/chocolate-chip-brioche/

BREAD MACHINE COOKBOOK

SheKnows Editors. (2018, March 20). *Your Handy Guide to Converting any Recipe to Gluten-free.* Taste of Home. https://www.tasteofhome.com/article/converting-recipes-to-gluten-free/

Shepard, J. (2020). Positively Perfect Gluten Free Pumpernickel. *GF Jules.* https://gfjules.com/recipes/positively-perfect-gluten-free-pumpernickel/?aff=5

Stroh, C. (2013a, July 28). Garlic Bread-Machine Bread Recipe [Vegan/Gluten Free]. *Make Real Food.* http://makerealfood.com/2013/07/28/garlic-bread-machine-bread-recipe-vegangluten-free/

The Ideas Kitchen. (2019, March 19). *Butternut Squash Breadmaker Soup.* https://www.theideaskitchen.co.uk/recipe/butternut-squash-breadmaker-soup/

Woodford, C. (2019, August 23). Bread Making Machines. *Explain That Stuff.* https://www.explainthatstuff.com/breadmaker.html

YourBreadMachine. (2017, September 4). Everything You Need To Know About Bread Machine and More. *Your Bread Machine.* https://yourbreadmachine.com/bread-machine-guide/#tab-con-2

Zojirushi. (n.d.). *Meatloaf Miracle.* https://www.zojirushi.com/app/recipe/meatloaf-miracle

Printed in Great Britain
by Amazon